Book Synopsis: "*God's Choreographers: Movement Geniuses*" is a specialized book that focuses solely on choreography for the Kingdom of God. This book will expand your revelation on this subject while empowering you to step into new realms of movement creativity. You will learn what choreography is, who choreographers are, various styles of choreography and more. The concept of movement geniuses will be unveiled as you dive into the complex mind of the choreographer. Each mind, process, and style is different. The revelation shared will encourage you in that difference. You will be empowered to be uniquely you and enlightened as to why it is crucial for you to rise up in this hour. You will learn your importance and be charged into action as God's choreographers who wreak havoc on the kingdom of darkness and build the kingdom of God on earth as it is in heaven! SHIFT!

(Website) Kingdomshifters.com

(Email) manifoldgrace5@gmail.com

(Email) kingdomshifters@gmail.com

Connect with Nina via Email, Facebook or YouTube

Copyright 2017 – Kingdom Shifters Ministries

All rights reserved. This book is protected by the copyright laws of the United States of America. This book may not be reprinted for commercial gain or profit. The use of occasional page copying for personal or group study is permitted and encouraged. Permission will be granted upon request.

Nina's Bio

Nina Cook has been saved since childhood and has been active in ministry much of her life. Nina carries an apostolic mantle with giftings in dance, singing, production, all manner of prayer, spiritual warfare, deliverance, healing, teaching, pastoring, scribing, and wellness. Nina graduated from Ball State University in 2014 with a Bachelor's Degree. She studied Exercise Science and minored in Dance. Nina has over five years of experience in the wellness and exercise field and 11 years and counting of dance experience.

Nina is an Elder at Kingdom Shifters Christian Empowerment Center in Muncie, Indiana. She is the main armor bearer for her pastor and is also training in her calling as an apostle. Nina is the founder of "Manifold Grace Production Company" and "Exercise to Life." It is her vision that her production company brings transformation to people and regions through the power and creativity of the arts. Nina is an extraordinary teacher and minister of movement, choreography, atmospheric worship, and using dance and movement in warfare and intercession. Nina provides fitness coaching and exercise and dance class through "Exercise to Life." She utilizes a vast variety of exercise and fitness styles that people can do that are combined with scriptural focuses, short teachings, prayers, and declarations and decrees such that when people do the exercises their bodies are transformed. It is her vision to see people transformed through bringing healing and deliverance to the physical body in areas that hinder their health and wellness, and to also see complete lifestyle changes that shift people into wholeness.

Nina is dedicated to living her life sold out to Christ. She is generally the first to volunteer and take risks for anything that grows the kingdom. She is always seeking to learn, develop, and cultivate herself in the integrity, character, fruit and will of God.

Connect with Nina and Manifold Grace Production Company at Manifoldgrace5@gmail.com, kingdomshifters.com *or via Facebook and Youtube.*

Table of Contents

Chapter 1 Movement Geniuses 1

Chapter 2 Why Are Choreographers Important? 7

Chapter 3 What Is Choreography & Who Are Choreographers? 13

Chapter 4 Styles of Choreography 17

Chapter 5 The Choreography Process ..28

Chapter 6 Be The Choreographer God Has Called You To Be Charge 46

Chapter 1

Movement Geniuses

You may be wondering why and how I came to the conclusion that God's choreographers are movement geniuses. This is not surprising because that is an abstract thought. However, I have lived it from a small child to the present time. The evidence of this statement in my life causes it to reign true. Are you ready to travel into the mind of God's choreographers and be enlightened to their unique complexity? Okay, let's dive in!

When I envision the mind of a choreographer, it is like looking into the brain activity of what I imagine a geniuses would look like. I can see the firing of the many neurons that communicate information throughout the different lobes of the brain and body; and the traveling signals lighting up in vast arrays of colors. Tons of creative ideas shooting off in the brain igniting a limitless flow of movement. One compartment speaking to another compartment, one idea adding on top of another idea. So forth and so on until a complete masterpiece is created and a new domain is hit and released onto the earth through the compilation of heaven establishing movement that is created.

Dictionary.com defines genius as "an exceptional natural capacity of intellect, especially as shown in creative and original work in science, art, music, etc." With the source of the gift being God, this exceptional ability is not natural but supernatural, being breathed into a person by the Spirit of God.

Einstein was a well-known genius who is responsible for creating the theory of relativity as well as many other theories and developments that has made his findings a pillar within modern physics. "Einstein always appeared to have a clear view of the problems of physics and the determination to solve them. He had a strategy of his own and was able to visualize the main stages on the way to his goal. He regarded his major achievements as mere stepping-stones for the next advance (nobelprize.org, 2018)." His mind enabled him to have clear view of both the problems and the solutions to solve them. As a genius, he was a visionary who could see the main goal and purpose while also being able to piece the small steps together that created the full work of advancement. This is why God's choreographers are geniuses. They see the main purpose of God's will and through their movement, they masterfully piece together a complete work that sets new foundations in lives and regions.

It is said that after Einstein died, they removed his brain for study purposes in hopes of finding what made his mind so brilliant. It is the creative building mind of the choreographer that makes them so profound. A genius is born and hardwired, their extraordinary intellect is not something that is attained although it can be heightened and sharpened through practice. Choreographers are geniuses because it is the nature of how their mind is made and works. They think differently, see differently, develop differently, each of them in a unique way to create movement that influences whatever is in their midst. Their movement is like an equation that provides the kingdom of heaven as the solution in the earth. Like Einstein, they are solution creators.

The movement of God's choreographers, does not come from the root of what looks good, what will make the people happy, or merely what would fit well with a great song. Their movement is breathed from supernatural realms, embodying the word, heart, will, character, nature, and power of God. The source of the breath (inspiration) is the difference between just a choreographer and God's choreographers who receive their inspiration from God's Spirit. They are not entertainers but establishers of the movement of heaven into the earth. Their purpose is not self-motivated, but fueled by God as they create movement to establish his will and not their own. They are always focused on the advancement of God's kingdom will.

> *2 Timothy 3:16-17 English Standard Version*
> *All Scripture is breathed out by God and profitable for teaching, for reproof, for correction, and for training in righteousness, that the man of God may be complete, equipped for every good work.*

As the movement is used for teaching, edifying and influencing people in the ways of God, it is breathed out just like the word. This makes the mind of the choreographer stretch beyond themselves to be one with the mind, heart, and Spirit of God. Their holy imagination must be in tune with his Spirit. What he pours out into them becomes what they spill out in their movement. They are exceptional in the original work they create directly from heaven itself. To be able to demonstrate the workings of an unseen realm and translate it into a reality takes a genius. It takes a supernatural capacity hand given and tailor made by God.

From a young age, I was always dancing and inventing my own dances. I would invent the dances, teach them to others, and even give them a name. On one occasion when I was about 4 years old, my grandmother came to visit for the Christmas holiday. She loved to play games, share stories, and dance with my brother and me. My mother loved to record us to document our childhood and she caught a video of me holding hands with my brother and my grandmother doing a dance and teaching them what it was. They asked "What is this dance called Nina?" In my 4 year old sweet raspy voice, I giggled and responded "the mashed potato." We all blew up in laughter and continued dancing and enjoying ourselves. I recall another video of me dancing the Macarena, a very popular line dance in the 90s and teaching it to all of my family members. During our family gatherings, everyone would always ask me to show them the new dance and of course I had and teach it to them. I would choreograph dances with my cousins and friends to perform for no reason beyond the fact that it was so much fun to me and just looking for an opportunity to dance.

The living room of my home was my studio. I danced in there so much that I wore out the carpet! That space was reserved just for me and my choreography. If my brother would come in, he would quickly be put out and come back from time to time to tease me and my friends if they were there. Choreographing was not a task or a work, but a natural passion, desire, and special place. Home you could call it. With my little stereo, tapes and CDs, countless dances were produced and the makings of one of God's choreographers began. The dances always did well and as I continued in building my gift, I only grew and flourished more and more.

Looking back on these events, I understand that this was a capacity imprinted in me since birth. Not only was I naturally a gifted dancer, but I had the natural ability of a leader who would teach others. All of the dancing and choreographing as a child was cultivating and equipping me to carry and walk in the supernatural dimensions of my God ordained calling that was beyond the natural. This gift was not for me but for the advancement of the kingdom of God.

As I have matured in my gift, I have recognized the intricacy of the mind of God's choreographers. We are not only creating movement and putting dancers together. We are creating heaven and bringing it to earth. The kingdom, will, and power of God are manifested right before the eyes of those who receive of our ministry. They may believe that what they have received was an awesome and powerful dance ministry. Yet, they have truly received an impartation from heaven and God's kingdom has infiltrated their lives and land through us.

Chapter 2

Why Are Choreographers Important?

You may have an important question at this point in the book and I have an answer. You may be thinking, "Why are choreographers important in the body of Christ?" "Aren't they just dancers?" They are indeed dancers, however, they have access to a creative dimension past the typical dancer who can learn and execute movement taught to them by others. They help the body of Christ see the importance of dance ministry because it is the movement that should demonstrate the word, power, character, nature, purity, holiness, and Spirit of God. The movement that the choreographer develops, differentiates the ministry of dance from the world, entertainers, or performers. The choreographer holds a great responsibility because it is the movement they create that determines if the church and viewers see and experience Christ. They help teach the body of Christ the true depths of dance ministry that displays not just gifts, but the actual callings and assignments of God that are on the lives of the ministers. If the choreographers are not skilled, how do we expect the body of Christ and world at large to honor, respect and receive us. If we are incorporating moves from the world, songs from the world, dancing sensually, or with out any purpose or biblical foundation as the basis of our movements, we are a detriment to ourselves. If the choreographers are not developed, they can play a critical role in the negative perceptions that many have towards the ministry of dance. This is why choreographers are important. Are they just dancers? No. They are the gateway to which the entire dance ministry is perceived. They form the reputation and virtue of the ministry. We need God's choreographers to arise, teach, and create movement that demonstrates and releases the true nature of God. As God's choreographers truly learn who they are, we will see a unexplainable shift in the body of Christ and world at large within this ministry.

The choreographer receives vision from God and they bring those realms of the kingdom into the earth by translating what they see and hear into movement. This is the difference between a dancer and a choreographer. A dancer receives vision from the choreographer to execute the movement and release the message of the choreography effectively. They are like a pupil receiving direction, and the choreographer is one who stands as a leader and teacher. This is one of the reasons why God's choreographers are important. They are the teachers, and this is a much needed function in this ministry. As they teach, they impart what God has revealed to them through the movement and instruct the ministers on how to demonstrate the word while making sure that Christ is formed in every region and person who receives of their ministry.

We need those who can receive direct vision from God through movement and skillfully lead others such that dance ministers are not merely dancing, but wreaking havoc on the kingdom of darkness bringing forth transformation, healing, deliverance, miracles, signs, and wonders. God's choreographers must know the power that rest within them so they can tap into creative streams of movement and realms in the heavenlies that have not been broken open yet. Those who know they are gifted in being able to create movement must shift forth from merely just dancing to opening up their spiritual imagination to create the word of God and teach movement that transforms people and regions.

We do not hear much about the concept of choreography in the kingdom of God. Although we are seeing a new arising of dancers and greater acceptance of this ministry within the body of Christ, there is still much ground breaking to be done. Dancers are being trained, but those who are choreographers need to be trained as well and enlightened to the depths of who they truly are as creators. When choreographers have a Moses moment like when God asks him "What is that in your hand?" And he threw it on the ground and numerous wonders came from it, we will see power demonstrated through dance like we have never imagined!

> ***Exodus 4:2-3 New Living Translation*** *Then the* L*ORD* *asked him, "What is that in your hand? "A shepherd's staff," Moses replied. "Throw it*

> *down on the ground," the* LORD *told him. So Moses threw down the staff, and it turned into a snake! Moses jumped back. Then the* LORD *told him, "Reach out and grab its tail." So Moses reached out and grabbed it, and it turned back into a shepherd's staff in his hand.*

Hand in that scripture from the Strong's concordance means "power, custody, strength, dominion, and border." God was asking him what is in your dominion. What is within you? God's choreographers must know the power that lies within them so that it does not remain dormant and such that they can utilize it effectively.

Choreography is so impactful that it marks and conjoins entire generations together. The 50's is known by dances such as the Jitterbug, Swing, the Bop, the Charleston, and the Lindy. The 70's and 80's are known for disco and pop dances. And the 90's is known for the evolution of hip hop dancing. These eras of unique dances drew tons of people together and remain an identifying force between those born in those time periods. With this understanding, God's choreographers can take over entire generations for the Kingdom of God. They can have major influence and draw people of all backgrounds to the culture of heaven which is eternal. There are no walls based on age, race, or nationality background. It is all about the movement of heaven that we all can connect to and unify with. The movement will have God's nature and character on it and separate between what is of him and what is not. A harvest of unity amongst his sons and daughters where all demographics of people can be liberated in who they are and in their praise and worship unto him will be yielded.

During the presidential term of Barack Obama, his wife Michelle Obama started a public health campaign called "Let's Move!" It's initiative was "solving the challenge of childhood obesity within a generation so that children born today will reach adulthood at a healthy weight." She targeted this issue and sought to bring forth change by using movement. Dance was one of the leading strategies she used to encourage children and even all people to get moving. This generation was greatly impacted by this campaign and by the movement that Michelle Obama has become known for. She appeared on numerous shows such as Ellen Degeneres, So You Think You Can Dance, and The Today Show. Her "Let's Move!" campaign traveled around the nation and is still impacting lives today. As movement geniuses, our influential power is limitless. Not only within the walls of the church, but even beyond that all around the world! We can capture the attention of many and impact lives, regions, and entire generations for the kingdom purposes of God through our choreography.

There is much talk of dance and choreography in the world and Hollywood. Michael Jackson, one of the most famous artist of our time created original signature moves that drew millions to him and that current artists are still trying to emulate because of his inspiration in their lives. Well known choreographers like Paula Abdul and Laurieann Gibson continue to be praised after years of service. We see shows like "So You Think You Can Dance" present works from choreographers who speak strong political and controversial messages through movement that inspire millions of viewers. As a result, it has become an award winning show. If this level of power and influence is in the hands of those who are not advancing the Kingdom of heaven, how much more impactful can God's choreographers be with heaven backing them!

The next chapter will take us even deeper in our understanding of why choreographers are important, as we dive into greater detail of who they are and what they do. Let's go!

Chapter 3

What Is Choreography & Who Are Choreographers?

Choreography is the process of composing and organizing movement in a specific form or pattern that molds into a dance sequence. It is also known as dance composition because it combines multiple movements to make a complete dance. Some of the words related to composition are structure, constitution and architecture. We can derive from these words that the process of developing choreography can be likened to building a framework that can stand and sustain on its own. The composition of the movements that come into a complete form, become a skillfully sculpted structure that create foundation for the people who receive of it. With music or without, with words or without, to a prayer or to a poem, the foundation of the movement alone should remain strong and effective.

Choreography is architecture. While researching on architects, I read a profound sentence that embodied the assignment of a choreographer. "The architect hired by a client is responsible for creating a design concept that meets the requirements of that client and provides a facility suitable to the required use (Wikipedia.org, 2018)."

My Breakdown of this profound sentence:

"The architect (**choreographer**) hired by a client (**God**) is responsible (**mandated**) for creating a design concept (**choreography**) that meets the requirements of that client (**will and purpose of God**) and provides a facility suitable to the required use (**durable and effective for those who partake of it**)."

This is the commission of God's choreographers! We are responsible for creating movement that epitomizes his will and is sufficient enough to carry it out and institute it in the earth.

While the movement itself is the architectural structure, choreographers are the wise master builders. The Greek word for architect is arkhitekton, meaning chief builder.

> *1 Corinthians 3:10 King James Version*
> *According to the grace of God which is given unto me, as a wise masterbuilder, I have laid the foundation, and another buildeth thereon.*

Grace is a distinct endowment of God that empowers and exerts supernatural force on a person to do a certain task in excellence. Choreographers have a wise master builder grace. Wise in this scripture means skilled, expert, forming the best plans and using the best means for their executions. When choreographers put movement together, it is done with a strategic plan that is the most fruitful and effective for the people, atmosphere, and region. Demonic principalities and powers are ancient ruler spirits that operate over entire communities, regions and nations. They administrate demonic plans that allow darkness and destruction to control regions. Strategic movement has the power to overthrow darkness and displace demonic principalities and powers.

Master builder means a chief constructor, architect, and the superintendent in the erection of buildings. They are the center leaders that start (erect) the structure and leave room for others to build upon. The word and will of God that is released through the movement builds a framework in the people's lives and regions. As they receive of the framework that has been imparted into them, they can take that foundation and build upon it in their own lives and regions thus advancing the kingdom.

> ***Matthew 7:24-27 English Standard Version***
> *"Everyone then who hears these words of mine and does them will be like a wise man who built his house on the rock. And the rain fell, and the floods came, and the winds blew and beat on that house, but it did not fall, because it had been founded on the rock. And everyone who hears these words of mine and does not do them will be like a foolish man who built his house on the sand. And the rain fell, and the floods came, and the winds blew and beat against that house, and it fell, and great was the fall of it."*

God's choreographers are different from the accustomed choreographer. We are not creating movement to be innovative and awe striking. Nor to produce a hype response in the people. We are creating movement to ignite transformation by the word and will of God that it releases. It is important that you use the word of God to build. Those who build with the word are wise. God's word always stands and accomplishes. As you seek God for the movement and build by what he reveals to you, your choreography will yield an eternal work. It will keep producing fruit in the people, atmospheres, and regions that you minister in. You are not just a choreographer. You are a architect and wise master builder. Now that you know who you are, I impute you to begin building dances from this dimension!

Chapter 4

Styles of Choreography

Every choreographer is different and has a style that is unique to the mantle and calling that is on their life. Their specific choreography skill is like their thumbprint of identification and leaves an individual imprint upon the atmospheres, people, and regions they impact. It expresses who they are and who God is in them. Their style communicates and establishes the mandate that is upon their life, the offices they may operate in if God has called them to one, the anointings they may flow in, and the distinct passions that God has placed in them.

Examples of this:

- ❖ A person who creates movement that frequently causes them to dance in the audience may have a strong heart for people. They may be evangelistic or pastoral. They may have a healing anointing that drives them to come into close proximity with the people so they can personally touch them and connect with them.
- ❖ A person who often creates movement that is very sharp, piercing, and have the ability to reach the hearts, souls, and minds of people and birth forth deliverance through their movement may be a choreographer that is strong in intercession and carry a mandate for deliverance.

- ❖ A person who creates movement that releases heaven and opens up portals and realms of the word and heart of God to reign upon a region, group of people or person may be strong in the prophetic and have a passion for the heart and revelatory word of God.
- ❖ A person who creates movement that exhibits warfare, shifting and governing over atmospheres, demolishing darkness and evil while establishing the kingdom and power of God may be an apostolic dancer or warrior.

As a choreographer, you will not and do not have to create movement from just one well. These examples were provided to enlighten you to the point that your style of choreography will reveal some finite things about your identity although you may be able to create and flow through multiple wells. This is one of the many extraordinary components of being a choreographer and why they are God's movement geniuses.

Style which is the method to which you develop and execute movement, is really synonymous with creativity. When you choose a style that was not given to you, you hinder the fullness of who you are and who God is in you. We do not need a duplicate of another persons style and creativity because God only created one of them and only one of you and we need the uniqueness of what God has placed in each you. When you operate from your God-given style and creativity, you collaborate and come into agreement with who God says you are. He is expressed in a new form in the earth that only you can unveil.

Style is not and should not be a hindering factor to any choreographer or dancer. You should strive to be uniquely you when both developing and ministering the movement God reveals. Natural rhythm and understanding of music and beats is not a necessity when dancing for the Lord. Technical training in Ballet, Jazz, Modern, and Contemporary is not a mandatory prerequisite for you to walk in your gift. God is the source and foundation. Whatever we lack, we have limitless access to through the Holy Spirit. If you feel you do not have natural rhythm, coordination, a graceful flow, or other desired attributes, God will give it to you as you submit to him and allow the Holy Spirit to dance through you. The mindset that rhythm or prior technical training is a requirement, restrains many from being the dancer they know God has called them to be. To compensate, some dancers commit to dancing in styles that do not require much rhythm or coordination. Some only utilize styles they feel comfortable with and others do not dance at all. They spend years negating this part of their identity because of what they feel they do not have. They become their own limitation in reaching full capacity and never tap into the supernatural power of God.

> *1 Corinthians 6:19* What? know ye not that your body is the temple of the Holy Ghost which is in

you, which ye have of God, and ye are not your own?

1 Corinthians 3:16 *Don't you know that you yourselves are God's temple and that God's Spirit dwells in your midst?*
John 14:26 *But the Comforter, which is the Holy Ghost, whom the Father will send in my name, he shall teach you all things, and bring all things to your remembrance, whatsoever I have said unto you.*

Romans 8:9 *You, however, are not in the realm of the flesh but are in the realm of the Spirit, if indeed the Spirit of God lives in you. And if anyone does not have the Spirit of Christ, they do not belong to Christ.*

Psalms 18:33 *He makes my feet like the feet of a deer; he causes me to stand on the heights.*

Psalms 144:1 *A Psalm of David. Blessed be the LORD my strength, which teacheth my hands to war, and my fingers to fight:*

Habakkuk 3:19 *The Lord GOD is my strength, And He has made my feet like hinds' feet, And makes me walk on my high places. For the choir director, on my stringed instruments.*

Philippians. 4:13 *I can do all things through Christ who strengthens me.*

2 Corinthians 3:17 *Now the Lord is the Spirit, and where the Spirit of the Lord is, there is freedom.*

Letting go of our need to control, fears, comfort zones, and insecurities is a crucial component to breaking through in this area. Negative thinking and words must be crushed. Expressions like "I can't" get planted in the atmosphere and earth, and we train ourselves to agree with subtle word curses.

> ***Proverbs 18:21*** *Death and life are in the power of the tongue: and they that love it shall eat the fruit thereof.*

> ***1 Peter 3:10*** *For the Scriptures say, "If you want to enjoy life and see many happy days, keep your tongue from speaking evil and your lips from telling lies.*

> ***James 3:5 New Living Translation*** *In the same way, the tongue is a small thing that makes grand speeches. But a tiny spark can set a great forest on fire.*

We have to commit to speaking the truth of God concerning who we are and using scripture to edify ourselves in confidence, boldness, and power in our identity and limitless abilities. Once we do this consistently and step out of our comfort zones, the fruit of the edification will be evident in our lives and ministry.

> ***Psalm 141:3*** *Set a guard, O LORD, over my mouth; Keep watch over the door of my lips.*

> ***Psalm 34:13*** *Keep your tongue from evil And your lips from speaking deceit.*
>
> ***Proverbs 15:4 New Living Translation*** *Gentle words are a tree of life; a deceitful tongue crushes the spirit.*

There are many dancers in my production company who have never taken technical dance classes nor would they classify themselves as natural dancers. Yet, when I teach them challenging moves, they master them quickly. They have been trained with the mindset that they can do all things and have been consistently built up in their confidence and unique identity. They may look at me with eyes of surprise as they think about themselves executing the movement, but they push forward and produce excellence in each dance. As others view our ministry and share how it has blessed them, many believe that each dancer has been trained technically. However, that is nothing but the Holy Ghost and God's manifold grace manifesting in power through the ministry.

In a traditional dance instruction class, the use of counting systems is a prevalent style. The progression of movement is formed in counts of 8, 16, or other count patterns. This forms repetition and gives the dancer a consistent pattern to remember the sequences of movement. This helps develop the mental memory of a dancer as well as their muscle memory. It trains the mind and body that every time the count pattern starts over, the next sequence of movement will begin. This may be an easier style for choreographers who have been trained like this. The entire dance follows this continual pattern and each movement has its own count.

With this style, you can also put emphasis on certain counts to accent that a certain expression and execution is to be placed on that movement. This would be something like, 1-**2**-3-**4**-5-**6**-7-**8**. The emphasis being put on the movements corresponding with the bold numbers. As the dancer keeps hearing this accentuation, this helps them remember to do the movement a certain way. It trains their body to react such that when you stop counting and allow them to dance by themselves, they still execute the movements with the correct emphasis. Once you begin using this style of choreography, your ear will be trained to hear music in this form. Even when you are just listening to music at home or in your car, you will easily identify where the counts of 8, 16 or etc. begin and the different changes that may occur during the song.

Written notation is another style of choreography. Also known as dance notation, this is a symbolic way of using graphic symbols, figures, path mapping, words, and numbers to layout a dance. This is not a very common style today and is commonly used for historical conservation of dances. With this information, a famous dance could be repeated or revamped in the future to be performed again.

I believe I have created my own form of dance notation that is unique to me. I tend to maximize my time by working on dances during my free time at work. From behind my desk, I am not able to do the movements full out or map the spacing with my body. I get floods of movement and in order to keep up and not forget the movements and ideas God shows me, I have to write them down. I use words and symbols that I would know so that I can remember precisely what God showed me. I even write down formations and transitions. My writings may not make much sense to others, but they make a lot of sense to me and allow me to capture the movements that God may reveal at any given time.

This is a very convenient style when:

- You are not able to dance full out.
- You are multitasking (doing normal daily duties but want to be productive in working on choreography).
- You are brainstorming through ideas and seeking God for movement revelation.
- You are receiving an intense flood of movement insight from the Lord and the only way you can catch it all and remember it is to write it down.

I use dance notation for each of these reasons and have found it to be very beneficial. Anyone can utilize this style if it is something that would help them in keeping track of all of their thoughts, ideas and movement visions.

The use of sound where the choreographer makes different beats and rhythms with their mouth to express the tempo, phrasing, and syncopation of the song and movement is another style of choreography. The tempo is the rapidity and rate of speed. Phrasing is the grouping of music in a distinct phase. Syncopation is the accenting of beats that would not normally be accented. A person who uses this style of choreography is typically highly musical. They may have studied music or they may just have an ear for sound. Instead of using counts they may make beats with their mouth to signify and articulate the execution and intensity of the movements. This style brings in another element of expression and creativity and reveals the musicality of a person. Meaning the person has a hyper sensitivity and talent in being able to hear music from a skillful ear. It is easier for a person using this style to sound out the beats because it is simply what overpowers them as they hear the music and see the movements. While others just hear a song, they can hear every little intricate detail. This style helps them express that and gives them the ability to draw others into being able to hear what they hear. As they engage in each sound they hear, they are able to choreograph movements to each component. Beats and rhythms that you have never heard come alive. These beats are often crucial to the ministry and allow the dance to do mighty works in the realms of intercession, warfare, and demolishing darkness. Although you do not have to utilize this style to do this.

You can ask God to give you this level of musical insight and spend time listening to music to practice deciphering between the different components of the song. This will grow your ear and choreographic skill tremendously. I am able to hear music to this degree and I recall one time when we were dancing praise and worship during an event a team member shared with me that she thought I was off beat during one of the songs. The drums were very heavy during the song and there were multiple beats going on between the musicians. We laughed and I shared with her that I was not off beat but could hear the back beat and that is the one I was ministering too. Since that time, she has been able to recognize the beats and encourages me in this area.

God may also lead you in a style of teaching exactly what you see and receive from him. As the leader, you may have a personal practice to prepare choreography before you meet with your team. Or you may choreograph with your team as you progress through the song that will be ministered. It is important to do both of these when working with a team. When we have a rapidly approaching ministry engagement, I will have a personal practice to prepare before I meet with the team. This way, the time is spent with them learning the choreography and not us all seeking God for movement and putting it together during the practice. However, you want to be cognizant of doing this all the time. Make sure that you trust your team and you are giving them an opportunity to learn and grow in their choreography skill. Take time to choreograph with your team often and give them a chance to help carry the vision of the dance with you. You do not want to have a team full of great dancers but no one who is cultivated in their ability to receive movement direction and creativity directly from God. You want to cultivate a team of leaders and creators. You may need their help in the future as your ministry expands and you are not capable of choreographing every single dance. Since you as the leader have the grace for choreography upon your life, every person that is a part of your team also has this grace. Lead and empower your team in this truth.

Each of these styles of choreography are useful. You may even have your own unique style that is not listed here. No matter what style you use, the finished product should be God breathed. Whether you count, write, or are skilled in sound, your movement should always embody the word and demonstrate the will and power of God. The style is simply how you put together what God reveals to you. It does not dictate how you hear from God or what you receive from heaven. In the next chapter, we will dive in deeper to learn about the choreography process as God's choreographers.

Chapter 5

The Choreography Process

> *Habakkuk 2:1-3 I will stand upon my watch, and set me upon the tower, and will watch to see what he will say unto me, and what I shall answer when I am reproved. And the LORD answered me, and said, Write the vision, and make it plain upon tables, that he may run that readeth it. For the vision is yet for an appointed time, but at the end it shall speak, and not lie: though it tarry, wait for it; because it will surely come, it will not tarry.*

This scriptural passage provides a clear description of the choreography process. Receiving movement from the Lord is like writing a vision of the word and will of God upon the hearts and minds of people, and upon the regions and territories we minister in. It is making it plain in them that they would be able to progress in the word being released.

<u>Stand</u> in the Strong's Concordance means:
1. To stand, remain, endure, take one's stand
2. Be in a standing attitude, present oneself, become a servant of
3. To tarry, remain, continue, abide, endure, persist, be steadfast
4. To station, set, maintain
5. To appoint, ordain, establish

To receive vision for movement from the Lord you must be correctly postured to receive from him. It is an established stance, attitude, and station that you remain in through the process. It is important that before you begin to work on choreography, you receive vision about the purpose of your ministry event. This way you can build a dance where each movement embodies that purpose and is not idle movement or a hosh posh of movement. If you truly are wanting to receive movement that serves the Lord and is not just pretty, good to look at, and hype, this stance to receive from him will cause you to be inspired by the Lord.

> ***2 Timothy 3:16*** *All scripture is given by inspiration of God, and is profitable for doctrine, for reproof, for correction, for instruction in righteousness:*

<u>*Inspiration* in the Strong's Concordance in this scripture means:</u>
1. Divinely breathed in
2. Inspired by God

<u>*Inspire* from Dictionary.com means:</u>
1. To fill with an animating, quickening, or exalting influence
2. To produce or arouse (a feeling, thought, etc.)
3. To fill or affect with a specified feeling, thought, etc.
4. To influence or impel
5. To communicate or suggest by a divine or supernatural influence
6. To guide or control by divine influence
7. To prompt or instigate by influence

8. To give rise to, bring about, cause, etc.

Choreography should be divinely breathed in by God. His exalting supernatural influence should be guiding, controlling, communicating, and producing his movement in us. Just as all scripture was given by the inspiration of God, as dance ministers, our choreography which is essentially our scripture, should be received by the inspiration of God.

Dictionary.com defines inspire as

1. to fill with an animating, quickening, or exalting influence:
2. to produce or arouse (a feeling, thought, etc.):
3. to fill or affect with a specified feeling, thought, etc.
4. to influence or impel
5. to animate, as an influence, feeling, thought, or the like
6. to communicate or suggest by a divine or supernatural influence:
7. to guide or control by divine influence.

Cultures who serve idol gods summon their gods which are demonic spirits to receive their inspiration. Kathak is an Indian classical dance inspired by the stories of the Hindu god Krishna. Kalilambe is an African dance symbolic of the celebration of harvest, life, and the birth of children. It is a ritual performed that worships fertility. Krump dance in the American culture is inspired by emotions of anger, rage, grief and loss, and release to reach a point of ecstasy. There are countless other dances around the world that are being inspired by demonic influence. It is important that dance ministers of God receive inspiration only from him and release the breath of God into the earth realm.

The scripture says that it is profitable for:

- Doctrine (instruction, teaching, learning) - Our choreography should teach, give instruction, and cause people to learn whatever God is speaking through our ministry.

- Reproof (proof, conviction, evidence) - Our choreography should embody evidence, proof of God and bring conviction.

- Correction (restoration to an upright or right state, improvement of life or character, reformation) - Our choreography should improve, restore, and reform the lives and characters of people.

- Instruction in righteousness (education or training, chastening, nurture, cultivation of minds, morals, and increasing virtue, integrity, purity, correctness of thinking, feeling, and acting) - Our choreography should educate, train and cultivate people in godliness.

The scripture ends by saying *"That the man of God may be perfect, thoroughly furnished unto all good works."*

Our choreography should bring perfection, solidification, and do a complete work in the people and regions that we minister too.

One of the ways I position myself to receive movement from the Lord is through prayer. Prayer is a posture of wanting to communicate with the Lord, as well as wanting to hear, see, and receive from him.

> ***Matthew 7:7*** *Ask, and it shall be given you; seek, and ye shall find; knock, and it shall be opened unto you:*

<u>Ask</u> in the Strong's Concordance in this scripture means:

1. To ask, beg, call for, crave, desire

You ask and call for God to show you his movement. Place before him your desire to receive choreography inspired by only him.

<u>Seek</u> in the Strong's Concordance in this scripture means:
1. To worship God, desire, endeavor, enquire for, require
2. To seek in order to find purposeful intentional direct
3. By thinking, meditating, reasoning
4. To seek after, aim at, strive after
5. To crave, demand something from someone

Spend time worshipping as you seek him for movement. Meditate in him, placing your mind, thoughts, and reasoning before him to be filled with his thoughts and plans. To seek in order to find means to be purposeful, intentional, and direct in what you are needing. Do not seek for just any movement. What you are seeking from God needs to be in alignment with the vision God is wanting you to release. This will make the vision of the dance clean and clear. Aim at, strive after, and put a demand on God to reveal his vision of movement.

Knock in the Strong's Concordance in this scripture means:
1. To rap
2. To knock at the door

Rap in Dictionary.com means:
1. To strike, especially with a quick, smart, or light blow
2. To utter sharply or vigorously
3. The sound produced by such a blow

You may have to war to breakthrough and receive movement.

- ❖ Speaking in fierce tongues while you are praying until there is a shift and breaking.
- ❖ Decreeing and declaring out the purpose of the dance.
- ❖ Praying over the people and region you will be ministering in - there may be demonic spirits connected to them that do not want them to receive what your ministry is releasing.
- ❖ Decreeing out scripture that aligns with the purpose of the ministry.

These are all strategies that can help you breakthrough to revelation and choreography.

Since you are aiming to create a visual of God's word through movement, the devil will send blockages because your movement will advance the kingdom.

When choreographing, you may experience blockages such as:

- ❖ You see nothing - white space or black space, emptiness. God revealed to us that this is called the spirit of void and darkness. Your eye gates, imagination, atmosphere, and mind are all blank, dark, and empty. *Genesis 1:2 The earth was without form and void, and darkness was over the face of the deep. And the Spirit of God was hovering over the face of the waters.*

- ❖ You will be executing movement one moment and the next moment it disappears from your mind and body. You cannot make progress because you keep forgetting the movement. This is called the zapping spirit. It strikes and jolts the movement from you. *John 10:10 The thief comes only to steal and kill and destroy. I came that they may have life and have it abundantly.*

- ❖ It will feel like you are being blocked from receiving movement. This is a blocking spirit. A wall, barrier, or troop of demons that have locked themselves together in the spirit realm to hinder you from forward motion. *Psalms 18:29 For by you I can run against a troop, and by my God I can leap over a wall.*

- ❖ You will feel confused, frustrated, disconnected from being able to understand and comprehend the movement. This is called the deaf and dumb spirit. It hinders your ability to see, hear, and fully grasp the movement. **Mark 4:12** *they may indeed see but not perceive, and may indeed hear but not understand, lest they should turn and be forgiven.*
- ❖ You do not receive anything because the song choice is not right.
- ❖ You might have good movements but they do not feel right. However, you cannot put your finger on it.

Using these tools of prayer will help you break through these attacks purposed to hinder your progression in choreographing.

Posturing to receive from God through prayer draws you near to him. It allows you to connect with him and his spirit, which shifts you inside of his presence and inside of the spirit realm. You ascend to the throne room of God to receive what you are praying for (Hebrews 4:16). When you come into the throne room, you become seated in heavenly places with Jesus. You cease from the thoughts, familiarities, and limitations of your own mind. This realm grants you access to heavenly movement that is unlimited in creativity and power. Movement that is beyond this earth.

> **Ephesians 2:6 King James Version** *And hath raised us up together, and made us sit together in heavenly places in Christ Jesus:*

Colossians 3:1-2 King James Version *If ye then be risen with Christ, seek those things which are above, where Christ sitteth on the right hand of God. Set your affection on things above, not on things on the earth.*

<u>Above</u> in the Strong's Concordance means:
1. Up, upwards, above, on high
2. Of the quarters of the heaven, northward
3. The word could refer to either place or time. Place- the Jerusalem which is above- in the heavens, time- the eternal Jerusalem which preceded the earthly one

You are seeking and receiving movement that is from above, on high, of the quarters of heaven.

<u>Affection</u> in the Strong's Concordance means:
1. Exercise the mind
2. To have understanding, be wise
3. To feel, to think
4. To have an opinion of one's self
5. To be of the same mind, agreed together, cherish the same views, be harmonious
6. To direct one's mind to a thing, to seek, to strive for

Receiving heavenly choreography from God is a state of mind. You must come into agreement and be harmonious with heaven. It is an exercise of the mind.

<u>Earth</u> in the Strong's Concordance means:

1. The ground, the earth as a standing place
2. The earth as a whole

3. The earth as opposed to the heavens
4. The inhabited earth, the abode of men and animals
5. A country, land enclosed within fixed boundaries, a tract of land, territory, region

Choreographing from an earthly stance limits you to the confines of man. You will only have access to what is fixed within the bounds of the land. The movements you have seen before, have done in the past, have received from other people, that are popular, will be the only movements you can see from an earthly perspective. When you set your state of mind on heaven becoming harmonious with it, you will bring the movement of heaven into the earth. Your choreography should fulfill the mandate of thy kingdom come, thy will be done on earth as it is in heaven. Choreography is not creating good moves, it is bringing the kingdom of heaven to earth through movement.

> ***Matthew 6:10 King James Version*** *Thy kingdom come. Thy will be done in earth, as it is in heaven.*

Each movement becomes a portal that connects heaven to earth, while releasing the royal authority and power of God to rule and reign in the lives of the people you are ministering to, and the regions and territories you are ministering in.

<u>*Come* in the Strong's Concordance in this scripture means:</u>
1. To come from one place to another
    - You translate heaven to earth.

2. To appear, make one's appearance, come before the public
   - You cause heaven to appear before the people.
3. To come into being, arise, come forth, show itself, find place or influence
   - You allow heaven to arise and find influence in the earth.
4. Be established, become known
   - Knowledge of the kingdom becomes established.

<u>Will</u> in the Strong's Concordance in this scripture means:
1. What one wishes or has determined shall be done
2. Of the purpose of God to bless mankind through Christ
3. Of what God wishes to be done by us- commands, precepts
4. Will, choice, inclination, desire, pleasure

We establish his commands, desires, and determinations as we embody his will in our movements.

<u>Done</u> in the Strong's Concordance in this scripture means:
1. Be brought to pass, be finished, be fulfilled
   - Doing a complete work of the will of God through your movement.
2. Be published, be ordained to, be married to

- Publishing, ordaining, and causing the will of God to marry earth.
3. To appear in history
    - Should do an eternal and lasting work, leaving a mark in the people and regions.
4. To be made finished- of miracles, to be performed wrought
    - The movement should produce the fruit of miracles and limitless possibilities of God.

Once this realm of heaven is open in your mind:
- You will be able to receive movements that are unique, different, and have not been seen before.
- You will know that the movements are from God because of its nature and the power that flows as you execute it.
- You will receive movement that has revelation of God's will, purpose, and meaning infused into it.
- You will receive downloads from heaven to establish in the earth.

Publishing heaven in the people and regions you minister to is like Habakkuk 2:2 says, *"Write the vision, and make it plain upon tables"*. Plain in this scripture means that you dig, engrave, declare, make clear the vision of God through your choreography. And the tables are like the people and regions that you engrave it upon.

You can tell when movements are not from God when:
- It is dry, dull, stagnant and stale – lifeless.
- There is no piercing or penetrating of the movement in the spirit.
- There is no power or fortitude to it - even slower more intimate moves should be filled with power.
- When it drags and lags behind - it feels like being in molasses.
- When the music drowns it out rather than it dominating and governing the music.
- When the movement is more of an improvising than actually fitting the song.
- When it entails sensual or sexual innuendos - it does not have the character of God.
- Has mixture and you can tell that there are worldly entanglements involved in it - lacks purity and holiness.
- Has more of a "look at me" feel rather than a "look at God" and what he is doing through the movement.
- It feels forced as if you had to come up with something more so than operating in the peace and flow of the Holy Spirit.
- You keep going over it but keep forgetting certain parts - you get to a part and it either does not flow or just feels out of place.
- You are hindered in choreographing further because that part is blocking true revelation from coming forth because it is not God's design.

My Choreography Process

I begin my process by praying and asking God what the focus of the dance is. I ask him questions like:

- ❖ What are the people supposed to be receiving from the dance?
- ❖ What hindrances may block them from receiving what will be released through the dance?
- ❖ What is the condition of the people's hearts, minds, inner-man, and spirit who we will be ministering to?
- ❖ What is the atmosphere of their church, ministry, and region?
- ❖ What demonic spirits will we be combatting, if any?

Depending on what you are ministering for, all of these questions may not be applicable. These are just some examples of the questions I ask and pray about, especially when ministering abroad and outside of my home church. As I take the time to pray into these questions, God gives me clear descriptive answers to each of these. Now that I have the focus, I search for scriptures that align with the purpose of the ministry. This fills the movement with the power of the word of God. It builds and empowers my spirit as I study and meditate on them consistently, as I go throughout the preparation process, and all the way up to the ministry engagement. Since I know the direction God is taking the dance, I begin to look for songs that embody the vision. The song has to be able to help me bring forth the movement in fullness, and bring in a shift. This can take a little time, and that is okay because you want to find the song that includes all of the aspects God revealed to you. If you like the song but you know that it is not the "one," it is okay to keep listening and praying. God will give you the song.

Sometimes we will even minister to two songs and combine them one after the other. This helps to do a complete work and bring about a solidification. For example, one song may be breaking bondages off of people, while the song after it will be filling them back up with freedom and healing. God will lead you in being able to deliver the whole message and bring the full vision to pass. As I listen to the song, movements that go along with the vision fill my mind and my body. There are times I receive movement like sparks of fire and other times it is like the erupting of a volcano. Back beats, undertones, syncopations, subtle rhythms and all types of things flow to the forefront of my mind. Sometimes I have to stop and think through everything that I am receiving. I like to make sure that I am incorporating every sound I hear into the dance because of what it may be ministering inside of the spirit realm. Others may have gone ahead of me to try to choreograph the next part but because of the level of download I may be receiving at the time, it can take me longer to process through it all and grasp the most effective movements. When working with my team we all laugh at the quirky things I do when processing through choreography. I may stop in silence as an entire movement movie plays in my spiritual vision. I may make beat sounds or tap my feet to accent the movements I am seeing, do variations of movement until I find the right one, or burst out in prayer so that we can break through. All of this is distinct to who I am and I have become confident in just being me, as this births the most genuine and effective product.

Going further into the process, sitting down at work listening to the song to prepare, I tend to envision movements. I jot down little notes to help me remember the moves for later when I can physically dance and activate the movements. Since I have already spent time in prayer, have clear descriptive vision, and filled myself with scripture, this part of the process can continue along with the flow. There will be times where you will have to pray through blockages as we discussed earlier in the chapter. It is always good to begin and end practice with prayer, whether it is personal practice or team practice. This helps to close you off from attacks and invites the Holy Spirit to reign and rain in your practice and move through your body.

When I get the chance to get up and dance, I piece together the movements that I saw in my mind. If they flow together when I minister them in my natural body, I keep them. If they do not, I try out different movements that go along with that section until I find the ones that fit. When I do not have movements coming to my mind, I dance around freely with God and I put together the movements that stick. If I am having trouble finding a move that brings out what the song is saying and/or what God is doing at that section in the dance, I will pull out my phone and use Dictionary.com to look up the definitions of the words in the song, or what I sense God is doing. I use the thesaurus as well to show me other words that describe it. This enhances my vision and aids me in being able to come up with unique and creative movement. One time we ministered a dance where the song kept repeating "God is going to blow your mind." So I looked up the word blow and it was no longer just blow, it was a sudden hard stroke with the hand and fist, a weapon, a hurricane, a strong breeze! My holy imagination was flooded with movement after receiving that revelation and having my vision enhanced. I came up with multiple creative and unique movements and the dance was powerful.

As the process continues, I try out different moves and take risks with my body, trusting the Holy Spirit. Some things work and some things do not, and that is okay. Taking leaps to launch out into creativity will help you to grow in your choreography skill and enlarge your arsenal of movement. This way, you will not be bound to repeating the same movements over and over. You can set your holy imagination free and give the Holy Spirit free reign to do things in your body that you have never done, and would have never thought you could do. Be okay to take risks, be creative, and let the Holy Spirit be limitless in you.

When I have developed a section of movement, I continue to build onto it until the dance is complete. In practice, as we minister the dance over and over we fine tooth comb through each movement and make sure that it is executed with power, precision, excellence, and genuine expression. The goal is not to merely do the movement, but to become the movement and embody the ability to plant it, reproduce it, and establish it.

Chapter 6

Be The Choreographer God Has Called You To Be Charge

Before reading this book if you have not been choreographing, dancing, or operating in your full capacity, you have passage into this ability. Ask God to pour out his spirit on you and open up your holy imagination and spiritual eyes for you to see his will and kingdom power through movements. Ask him to give you the ability to take what you see and translate it into a reality such that you not only see the movement, but you have the skill to grasp them and bring them into effect in the earth. Ask him to cultivate you in the distinction of who you are as his choreographer and fill you with the revelation and knowledge of what you bring to the earth through your choreography.

Every mind is different which makes the development of choreography all the more beautiful, unique, and powerful when in the hands, purposes and will of God. Seek to have God's thoughts, eyes, ears and heart as you choreograph. This will help you in producing his will through movement because you will be one with him. Trust that endless creative ability already lives in you. You were made in the image and likeness of God, thus, creativity is in your DNA.

God has anointed and appointed you to create. He mandated us to have dominion over all of the earth and establish his kingdom. There is no way to do this without the endowment of a creator. The words we preach create, our words create, songs create, prophesy creates and so on. There is nothing inferior about the power to create through dance. In fact, dancers breach, break up the ground, and create a path such that many of the other gifts can flow freely.

Rise up and know who you are! Rise up as a wise master builder and construct what God has shown you! Your impact and input is not too small but it is mighty. It wreaks havoc on the kingdom of darkness. It is clever, skilled, and strategic. I decree you will be undetected by the enemy and you will remain hidden and invisible, but the impact of your movement will not. As you go forth, you will see the impact and fruit of your labor. You will see the manifestations of what you have built and produced in people, regions, and atmospheres in abundance. God will blow your mind as you give him your mind. As you allow him to fill your holy imagination with limitless floods of his insight, heavenly vision, and supernatural movement wisdom. You will surprise yourself and receive a stream that you have never had before. Your movement will come with ease and you will be able to translate exactly what you see from heaven into effective and producing movement.

I decree there will be no blockages to you rising up in the truth of who you are. May you be positioned in confident boldness in your identity, as an eternal crushing of control, comfort zones, fear and insecurity has taken place as you have feasted on the revelation of this book. You are and will be the choreographer that God has called you to be. You are his movement genius. You are his thumbprint, imprint, and blueprint upon the earth. You are his skilled architect and one whom he has entrusted the task of building his kingdom in the earth. You are distinct, unique, tailor made and a rare representation of the image of God in the earth. You are special, uncommon and quirky and that is okay.

May you be filled with peace to be you and nothing less. I decree you are agreeing and aligning with exactly who God called you to be and a new capacity and grace is filling you. Your dances will be completed quicker and with ease. Creative sparks and volcanoes will erupt as you seek God for movement. As a leader, you will cultivate those in your care in being greater choreographers and dancers. Your labor will bless you, your team, ministries, regions, and generations to come!   Rise up and charge forth! You are **God's Choreographers: Movement Geniuses! SHIFT!**

References

Albert Einstein - Facts. (n.d.). Retrieved 2018, from https://www.nobelprize.org/nobel_prizes/physics/laureates/1921/einstein-facts.html

Dictionary.com. (n.d.). Retrieved 2018, from http://www.dictionary.com/

The Olive Tree Bible App by Olive Tree Bible Software. N.p., n.d. Web. 2018.

Strong, James. *Strong's Exhaustive Concordance of the Bible.* **Abingdon Press, 1890. Print**

Wikipedia.com. (n.d.). Retrieved 2018, from https://www.wikipedia.org/

Kingdom Shifters Books & Apparel

Available at Kingdomshifters.com

BOOKS FOR EVERYONE

Healing The Wounded Leader
Kingdom Shifters Decree That Thang
There Is An App For That
Kingdom Watchman Builder On the Wall
Embodiment Of A Kingdom Watchman
Dismantling Homosexuality Handbook

Releasing The Vision
Feasting In His Presence
Kingdom Heirs Decree That Thing
Let There Be Sight
Atmosphere Changes (Weaponry)
Apostolic Governing
Apostolic Mantle
Dancing From Heaven to Earth
Annihilating Church Hurt

BOOKS FOR DANCERS

Dancers! Dancers! Decree That Thang
Spirits That Attack Dance Ministers & Ministries
Dance & Fivefold Ministry
Dancing From Heaven To Earth

CD'S

Decree That Thing CD
Kingdom Heirs Decree That Thing CD
Teachings & Worship CD's

www.ingramcontent.com/pod-product-compliance
Lightning Source LLC
Chambersburg PA
CBHW061259040426
42444CB00010B/2429